S0-BPT-124

To

From

It's Your Birthday!

Compiled by
Lois L. Kaufman

Designed by Arlene Greco

Peter Pauper Press, Inc.

WHITE PLAINS, NEW YORK

All photographs licensed by The Image Bank®
The photographs appear
in the following sequence:
Endpapers © Carlos Navaja, "Roses" ©
Michael Melford, "Pink Rose with Water
Droplet" © Antony Edwards, "Yellow/Pink
Rose" © Philip De Renzis, "Close-Up of White
Roses" © Pat Lacroix, "Roses" © Joanna
McCarthy, "Rose" © Shoji Yoshida, "Bouquet
of Red Roses" © Harald Sund, "Rose" © Shoji
Yoshida, "Yellow Rose" © Pete Turner,
"Orange Rose - Detail" © Philip De Renzis.

Compilation copyright © 1998
Peter Pauper Press, Inc.
202 Mamaroneck Avenue
White Plains, NY 10601
ISBN 0-88088-836-9
Printed in China
7 6 5 4 3

It's Your
Birthday...

Have a happy one!

Oh! Life is so full and rich.

PEARL BAILEY

*To be astonished is one of
the surest ways of not growing
old too quickly.*

COLETTE

*Our birthdays
are feathers in the broad
wing of time.*

JEAN PAUL RICHTER

*I would rather
sing one day as a lion than
100 years as a sheep.*

CECILIA BARTOLI

*Believe in life!
Always human beings will
live and progress to greater,
broader and fuller life.*

W. E. B. DuBois

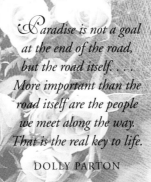

*Paradise is not a goal
at the end of the road,
but the road itself. . . .
More important than the
road itself are the people
we meet along the way.
That is the real key to life.*

DOLLY PARTON

*Live all you can;
it's a mistake not to.
It doesn't so much matter
what you do in particular,
so long as you have your life.
If you haven't had that,
what have you had?*

HENRY JAMES

Then came the time, when,
inseparable from one's own
birthday, was a certain sense
of merit, a consciousness of
well-earned distinction, when
I regarded my birthday as a
graceful achievement of my
own, a monument of my
perseverance, independence,
and good sense, redounding
greatly to my honour.

CHARLES DICKENS

I should have no objection to go over the same life from its beginning to the end: requesting only the advantage authors have, of correcting in a second edition the faults of the first.

BENJAMIN FRANKLIN

The best is yet to come.
I am going to live to be
one hundred . . . and I am
going to go on learning.

SHIRLEY MacLAINE

Every new day is as important as yesterday.

ELIZABETH TAYLOR

There is more to life than increasing its speed.

MAHATMA GANDHI

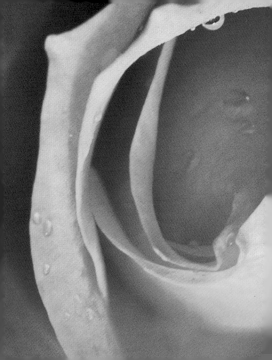

One must never,
for whatever reason,
turn his back on life.

ELEANOR ROOSEVELT

*The secret of a
happy life is to accept
change gracefully.*

JIMMY STEWART

I like adulthood to the extent that I'm more free to be a child.

MIKE MYERS

*Anyone who keeps
the ability to see beauty
never grows old.*

FRANZ KAFKA

When I was 14, I was the oldest I ever was. . . . I've been getting younger ever since.

SHIRLEY TEMPLE BLACK

All of us, until age four or five, see ourselves as the center of the universe. Some of us outgrow it. Some of us don't.

TONY CURTIS

*Nobody gets to live
life backward. Look ahead—
that's where your future lies.*

ANN LANDERS

Life isn't a matter of milestones but of moments.

ROSE KENNEDY

*A*s I have discovered
by examining my past,
I started out as a child.

BILL COSBY

You've got to look in the mirror and go, "This is reality, and it's all right."

LINDA RONSTADT

*If you live long enough
and fight hard enough,
a sense of comforting
continuity comes.*

MYRNA LOY

The secret of staying young
is to live honestly, eat slowly,
and lie about your age.

LUCILLE BALL

*Life itself is
the proper binge.*

JULIA CHILD

*You grow up the day
you have your first
real laugh at yourself.*

ETHEL BARRYMORE

Life is amazing, life is odd.
Life is not what
you expected it to be.
Things happen . . .
Growing up takes longer
than you think.

LAUREN BACALL

I am at one with the little invisible beings in the air— they who had begun as blue Flax flowers. The song is more joyous in youth, fuller and stronger in middle age; it quavers a little as the years go on and on: but the song itself is never ended.

KATE DOUGLAS WIGGIN

When I was a boy of fourteen, my father was so ignorant I could hardly stand to have the old man around. But when I got to be twenty-one, I was astonished at how much he had learned in seven years.

MARK TWAIN

*Every age can
be enchanting . . .*

BRIGITTE BARDOT

It takes a long time
to grow young.

PABLO PICASSO

*O*ne of the strange things
about living in the world is
that it is only now and then
one is quite sure one is going to
live forever and ever and ever.

FRANCES HODGSON BURNETT,

The Secret Garden

I have faith in my star,
that is that I am intended to
do something in the world.

SIR WINSTON CHURCHILL

*There is a fountain
of youth: it is your mind,
your talents, the creativity you
bring to your life and the lives
of people you love. When you
learn to tap this source, you
will truly have defeated age.*

SOPHIA LOREN

*For years I wanted to be
older, and now I am.*

MARGARET ATWOOD

Try to find something that needs to be done that only you can do.

MARGARET MEAD

*If you continue to
work and absorb the beauty
in the world, you find
that age does not necessarily
mean getting old.*

PABLO CASALS

Life is raw material.
We are artisans.
We can sculpt our
existence into something
beautiful . . .

CATHY BETTER

Youth is a quality, not a matter of circumstances.

FRANK LLOYD WRIGHT

*The less routine
the more life.*

AMOS BRONSON ALCOTT

*Every man's life is a fairy
tale written by God's finger.*

HANS CHRISTIAN ANDERSEN

Life loves to be taken by
the lapel and told: "I'm with
you kid. Let's go."

MAYA ANGELOU

*Life consists not in holding
good cards but in playing
those you hold well.*

JOSH BILLINGS

*It is not how many years
we live, but rather
what we do with them.*

EVANGELINE CORY BOOTH

*Let us live
while we live.*

PHILIP DODDRIDGE

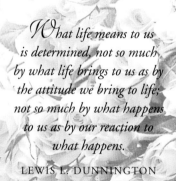

*What life means to us
is determined, not so much
by what life brings to us as by
the attitude we bring to life;
not so much by what happens
to us as by our reaction to
what happens.*

LEWIS L. DUNNINGTON

Some people go through
life trying to find out what
the world holds for them only
to find out too late that it's
what they bring to the world
that really counts.

LUCY MAUD MONTGOMERY

Be glad of life because it gives you a chance to love and to work and to play and to look up at stars.

HENRY VAN DYKE

*M*ay you live as long as
you want and not want as
long as you live.

TOM HANKS

*Life is a great big canvas,
and you should throw all the
paint on it you can.*

DANNY KAYE

*W*e all live in suspense
from day to day; in other
words, you are the hero
of your own story.

MARY McCARTHY

Dance like no one is watching,
Love like you'll never be hurt,
Sing like no one is listening,
Live like it's heaven on earth.

WILLIAM PURKEY

*Can't nothing make
your life work if you ain't
the architect.*

TERRY McMILLAN

May you live all the days of your life.

JONATHAN SWIFT

Three keys to more abundant living: caring about others, daring for others, sharing with others.

WILLIAM A. WARD

The way to keep young is to keep your faith young. Keep your self-confidence young. Keep your hope young.

LUELLA F. PHELAN

*Take care of the minutes,
and the hours will take
care of themselves.*

LORD CHESTERFIELD

*The greatest pleasure
in life is doing what
people say you cannot do.*

WALTER BAGEHOT

*Whatever with the
past has gone,
The best is always yet
to come.*

LUCY LARCOM

*Time has a
wonderful way of
weeding out the trivial.*

RICHARD BEN SAPIR

*Pleas'd to look forward,
pleas'd to look behind,
And count each birthday
with a grateful mind.*

ALEXANDER POPE

*Don't just count your years,
make your years count.*

ERNEST MEYERS

*Youth is a gift of nature,
but age is a work of art.*

GARSON KANIN

*The golden age is before us,
not behind us.*

ST. SIMON

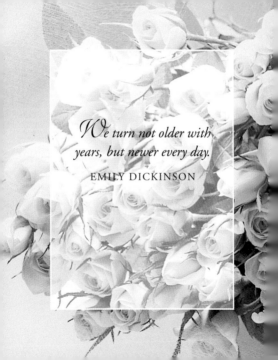

We turn not older with years, but newer every day.

EMILY DICKINSON

I'm still buying green bananas! I guess that makes me an optimist. Don't worry about me . . .

SARAH DELANY

(at 107)

*Every day is a birthday;
every moment of it is new
to us; we are born again,
renewed for fresh work
and endeavor.*

ISAAC WATTS